EMILY DICKINSON IN AMHERST

A GUIDE

By Jill Marion Maney

Illustrated by Allison Gosney

Published by
THE COMPUTER LAB
Box 4300
Ketchum, Idaho 83340

FAMOUS FOOTSTEPS™

guide booklets
about famous people
in their favorite places

Titles available:

Emily Dickinson in Amherst

Ernest Hemingway in Idaho

Ernest Hemingway in Key West

Georgia O'Keeffe in New Mexico

Mark Twain in the USA

Tennessee Williams in Key West and Miami

Front cover photo: Daguerreotype of Emily Dickinson, late 1847 or early 1848, at Mount Holyoke. Reproduced by permission of the Trustees of Amherst College.

Back cover photo: The retouched daguerreotype of Emily Dickinson. Reproduced by permission of Houghton Library at Harvard University.

ISBN 0-929-70905-5

First Edition

printed by
Sun Litho
USA

TABLE OF CONTENTS

NOTE TO READERS

I hope readers will find this brief guide to Emily Dickinson in Amherst helpful. Interest in Dickinson has increased since the centennial of her death in 1986.

Emily Dickinson is one of America's most important poets. Although few of her poems were published during her lifetime, in the years after her death relatives and scholars discovered drafts in drawers and around the Dickinson home which yielded over 1,700 poems. These are collected in *The Complete Poems*, edited by Thomas H. Johnson. Dickinson's poetry, letters, and accounts of her life are available at local bookstores, such as the Jeffery Amherst, the Golliard, Bookmarks, and the Albion Bookshops.

Amherst was the center of Emily Dickinson's life. She was born here, and although she travelled to other cities in her youth, she chose to return to Amherst, and she died here in 1886. In the poet's lifetime, Amherst was a village of 3,000, but also an important literary center and a growing industrial concern. Visitors arrived by horse and carriage or by the railroad that Edward Dickinson brought to the town. Emily Dickinson described the train in her poem, "I like to see it lap the miles." Today's visitor can reach Amherst on the same railroad. For information call Amtrak at 1-(800)-872-7245.

My personal interest in Dickinson grew during my undergraduate years at Amherst College, when I first was able to visit the places described here.

Many people have contributed time and energy to this project. I would like to thank my husband Jonathan, for his support and helpful criticism, my editor Marsha Bellavance-Johnson, who first envisioned the project and made it possible, Harold Johnson, who drafted the map of Amherst, and Lee Bellavance, for her editing work. Daniel Lombardo and Martly Noblick, of the Jones Library, John Lancaster, of the Robert Frost Library, Elaine Trehub and Patricia Albright, of the Williston Library, Carol Birtwistle at the Homestead, and Doug Wilson of Amherst College, were always helpful and enthusiastic. Finally, I want to thank the Trustees of Amherst College, and Houghton Library at Harvard University, for their kind permission to reproduce photographs of Dickinson and quote from her work.

INTRODUCTION

Emily Dickinson was born on December 10, 1830 in Amherst, Massachusetts, the second child of Edward and Emily Norcross Dickinson. She became one of America's greatest poets.

The Dickinson name had long been a center of attention in Amherst. Samuel Fowler Dickinson, Emily's grandfather, was a founder of Amherst College in 1821; her own father, Edward Dickinson, was a distinguished lawyer, politician, and even (for one term) United States Representative. Her brother Austin followed his father, becoming a lawyer, treasurer of Amherst College, and civic leader in the town.

Emily Dickinson enjoyed an active, social, and rather privileged childhood. Although she travelled in her early years to cities as far away as Washington and Philadelphia, Dickinson lived out her life in Amherst. She took fewer and fewer excursions as she grew older, and by the time she was forty, she had withdrawn almost completely. Amherst was an important town in Dickinson's lifetime; bigger than Concord, it was something of an intellectual center, with such notables as Ralph Waldo Emerson and Matthew Arnold coming to lecture there. There were also examples of successful literary women in town: Helen Hunt Jackson (see page 25), who went to school with Dickinson, became a best-selling novelist, coast-to-coast traveller, and crusader for Native American rights. Emily Fowler Ford, another classmate of Dickinson's, published a book of poems, *My Recreations*, in 1872, and had previously written essays, stories, and a successful biography of her grandfather, another Amherst resident, Noah Webster.

If Emily Dickinson's literary milieu was impressive, so was her education. The education she received was one of the best available to women in the country. After early elementary schooling at the brick schoolhouse on Pleasant Street, Dickinson's formal education commenced at Amherst Academy on September 7, 1840. The Academy stood on Amity Street near downtown Amherst; it is gone now, but the site is marked by a plaque (see map). The curriculum in Dickinson's time was very rigorous, and classes were coeducational. In his history of the Academy, Frederick Tuckerman writes that it was "a school successful beyond their most sanguine expectations, with a superior corps of teachers. . .second to none in New England."

Dickinson was an excellent student. After finishing her seventh year at the Academy in August of 1847, Dickinson was admitted to Mount Holyoke Female Seminary (see page 19). She encountered there an impressive female model: Mary Lyon, the founder of the school. Academics were stressed, and the curriculum was varied and difficult.

Dickinson spent a total of ten months, or two terms, there. Except for a childhood portrait now hanging in the Homestead, the only likeness of Emily Dickinson (shown on the front cover) was taken while she was at Mount Holyoke. In the years after her death, as the romantic version of the "poetess" was developed, the daguerreotype was retouched with frills and curls (see back cover).

Much speculation has arisen concerning Dickinson's reason for leaving Mount Holyoke. Certainly she had problems with illness; one severe bout of the flu sent her home for weeks. There is evidence that she was homesick, that her father wanted her home. Her sister Lavinia later claimed that Emily hated the place, but Dickinson's letters indicate that her feelings about Mount Holyoke were not all negative: "I love this seminary, & all the teachers are bound strongly to my heart by ties of affection." Perhaps more significant is the fact that her education at Amherst Academy may have duplicated that available to her at Mount Holyoke (many of the same textbooks were used), and the religious atmosphere at Mount Holyoke may have been somewhat overwhelming. Although the school was nonsectarian, a significant number of the students were preparing to become missionaries.

The school was experiencing what much of the surrounding countryside was in the mid 1800's--a religious revival. While conversion was never required or coerced, Mary Lyon strongly encouraged her students to convert. Emily Dickinson was among the few who did not profess religion. When Lyon divided the student body into three categories: "Christians" (those who had converted), "Hopers" (those who had hope of conversion), and "No-Hopers" (those who had no hope of becoming Christian), she placed Emily Dickinson in the last category. From school Dickinson wrote that many of her friends had been converted, but ". . . it is hard for me to give up the world." A year later, home from Mount Holyoke, she wrote, "I am standing alone in rebellion."

One by one, conversion touched each member of the Dickinson family. Emily Norcross Dickinson had converted in 1831. Edward professed faith in August 1850, Lavinia followed in November; Austin joined in January of 1856. Revival spirit also touched Emily Dickinson's friends: her beloved Abiah Root and Jane Humphrey both succumbed. Emily alone resisted.

Finished with school, faced with the examples of others around her as choices for her life--get married, convert, have children, become an educator like Mary Lyon, or rebel publically and write like Helen Hunt Jackson--Emily Dickinson chose to stay at home.

She also chose to become a poet. Starting tentatively at first, she wrote at her writing table, in the kitchen, on the back of bills and envelopes, at increasingly pitched pace and volume, until she had written an opus of 1,775 verses. Dickinson's earliest surviving poem is a valentine written when she was 20.

During the time that Dickinson was writing, she kept an extensive garden and cultivated exotic flowers in her conservatory. Surrounded by scientists like Edward Hitchcock at Amherst Academy and Amherst College, Dickinson became an expert in botany. Dickinson also devoted much of her time to nursing her invalid mother, and shared domestic duties with her sister Lavinia. Dickinson maintained a varied correspondence with many friends and relatives, both in Amherst and farther afield, that provided her contact with the world beyond "my Father's ground" and enabled her to share poems with others. Her correspondents included such prominent figures as Samuel Bowles, the editor of the *Springfield Republican*, and Thomas Wentworth Higginson, a writer for the *Atlantic Monthly.* A particularly interesting group of letters are those that Dickinson began "Dear Master"; the identity of the "master" remains a mystery.

Emily Dickinson's poems come to us now in many forms, from the edition of *The Complete Poems* edited by Thomas Johnson, to various selections of her work, often bound with illustrations. The story of how the poems came to be published is, however, a complicated one.

Fewer than a dozen of Dickinson's poems were published during her lifetime. Of the few that appeared in such places as the *Springfield Republican*, most were printed anonymously. Family and close friends knew that Dickinson wrote poetry, but few suspected it was her vocation. When her sister Lavinia found some of the poems in a drawer after Dickinson's death, many of them sewed into small collections or "fascicles," she was surprised by their number and impressed by their importance. Lavinia knew they should be published, but she was not in a position to publish them herself.

There were two women in Amherst who could help her. One was Susan Gilbert Dickinson, an old friend of Emily Dickinson's, married to her brother Austin, and living next door at the Evergreens (see page 21). The other was Mabel Loomis Todd, the wife of an Amherst professor of Astronomy, and friend of Thomas Wentworth Higginson. He was an important literary figure and a writer for the *Atlantic Monthly*. Dickinson had sent some of her poems to Higginson, and they continued to correspond until her death.

Lavinia went first to Susan Gilbert Dickinson. Susan was family, and Lavinia knew that Emily had shared some poems with Susan earlier in their lives. Lavinia gave about half of Emily's 1,775 poems to Susan, who promised she would try to publish them. Even after several years had passed, Susan did nothing. We can only speculate about why, but some scholars suggest that Susan's inaction had to do with that other literary figure in Amherst, Mabel Loomis Todd.

Mabel Loomis Todd was born in Cambridge, Massachusetts in 1856, and was raised in the cosmopolitan atmosphere of Washington D.C. In 1879 she married David Peck Todd, a former student of Amherst College. Together the two came to Amherst in 1881, when David Todd became a professor of Astronomy and Director of the Observatory at Amherst College. The young couple were soon "taken up" by Austin and Susan Dickinson. All went well at first, but by 1882, Mabel had begun an affair with Austin that lasted until his death. Mabel and Austin often met at the Dickinson Homestead, and Lavinia and Emily were somewhat complicit in the affair. It is uncertain how much Susan knew about the affair; certainly she did nothing about publishing Dickinson's poems.

Considering Susan's lack of action, Lavinia gave the rest of her sister's poems to Mabel Loomis Todd. Todd's reaction was swift. Although she had never met Emily Dickinson face to face, she was quick to recognize the excellence of her poems. She enlisted the help of Thomas Wentworth Higginson, their mutual friend, and the two of them published the first volume of Emily Dickinson's poetry in November of 1890. A second volume followed in 1891, and before the third volume appeared in 1896, Emily Dickinson's poetry was receiving international attention.

After Mabel's death in 1932, Millicent Todd Bingham carried on her mother's work. With her mother, Millicent edited *Bolts of Melody: New Poems of Emily Dickinson*, and on her own wrote *Ancestor's Brocades: The Literary Debut of Emily Dickinson*, *Emily Dickinson, A Revelation*, and *Emily Dickinson's Home*. These books are available at the Robert Frost Library (see page 31) or the Jones Library (see page 29).

Millicent Todd Bingham was not alone in continuing her mother's work. Susan Dickinson's daughter, Martha Dickinson Bianchi, collected and published Emily Dickinson's work from manuscripts given to her mother. She edited *The Single Hound*, an edition of Dickinson's poems published in 1914, and also *Emily Dickinson Face to Face: Unpublished Letters With Notes and Reminiscences*, and she wrote *The Life and Letters of Emily Dickinson.*

Today, Emily Dickinson's manuscripts are still divided. The Todd manuscripts reside at Amherst College, many of which are kept in Special Collections at the Robert Frost Library (see page 31), and the remainder of the Dickinson manuscripts are housed at Harvard.

Emily Dickinson died on May 15, 1886, after months of illness, from complications of Bright's disease. Her funeral was simple; she was buried in the family plot in West Cemetery (see page 27). Immediately after her death, interest in the poetry and the figure of Emily Dickinson grew. The Jones Library's bibliography on Emily Dickinson, published in 1930, indicates the range of this interest. Articles in such diverse newspapers as the *Oregonian* of Portland, Oregon, the *New York Times*, the *Philadelphia Inquirer*, and the *San Francisco Chronicle* show that interest spread nationwide. From the titles of some of these articles, it is easy to see how rumors about Dickinson devolved into myth: "Our Poetical New England Nun," "Poet, Mystic, Martyr," and "Emily Dickinson's Real Lover Revealed." Of course, these myths and rumors do little justice to what sustains our interest in Dickinson: the poems. Now that we have access to all 1,775 of them, with Dickinson's original punctuation restored, we can begin to know the real Emily Dickinson, a great American poet.

ALLISON GOSNEY
©'89

AMHERST COLLEGE

Amherst College was founded in 1821. One of its primary founders was Samuel Fowler Dickinson, Emily's grandfather. Already a successful attorney and state representative, in his later life Samuel Fowler Dickinson expended most of his time and almost all of his personal finances in realizing his dream of "the college on the hill." Townspeople saw it as an institution that would pursue a rigorous academic curriculum, but above all train young men in the Trinitarian religious tradition--a conservative school that would combat the "Unitarian heresy" at Harvard.

Amherst College has been in continuous operation since its founding, and has become one of the leading institutions of liberal arts education in the country. In Dickinson's time, it remained a center of the town, and of the Dickinson family. Emily's father, Edward Dickinson, was treasurer of the college, and was in large part responsible for its success. Austin Dickinson, Emily's brother, became treasurer after his father. In that office, he supervised the landscaping of the campus and construction of new buildings.

The Dickinson family reception was a fixture of commencement week at the college; Emily Dickinson herself hosted and entertained many graduates. Many of her friends were students at Amherst, such as her cousin John Graves, Henry Vaughn Emmons, and George Gould.

The campus has changed since Emily Dickinson's time, but many buildings look much the same. College Hall, at the corner of South Pleasant Street and Route 9, is a good example. A yellow Greek revival building with white columns, College Hall was completed in 1829 as the First Congregational Church. Here Emily Dickinson attended church with her family. College Hall was sold to the college in 1867, when a new First Church was built (see page 23).

Maps of the campus and tours are available at the Admissions Office, just off South Pleasant Street. Call (413) 542-2328 for more information.

ALLISON
©'89

THE DICKINSON HOMESTEAD

The Dickinson Homestead is located at 280 Main Street in Amherst. Emily Dickinson's grandfather, Samuel Fowler Dickinson, built the brick house in 1813. Its high ceilings, double parlors, and large bedrooms spoke of success.

The Dickinsons' tenure in the house was not to be secure, however. Not long after its construction, Samuel Fowler Dickinson's devotion to Amherst College left him near financial ruin: as Cynthia Griffin Wolff writes, "The Old Squire had mortgaged everything he owned." A complex arrangement with creditors ensued, and in 1830, Samuel Fowler Dickinson moved his family into the east half of the house, and his son Edward Dickinson and his wife moved into the west half. Here, with the property line running down the middle of the central entry hall, Emily Dickinson was born on December 10, 1830. Her sister Lavinia followed on February 28, 1833. Facing failure at home, Samuel Fowler Dickinson left Amherst for Ohio. In 1833 the entire Homestead was sold to Deacon David Mack of Amherst. Edward Dickinson and his family remained in the house until April 1840, when they moved to a frame house on North Pleasant Street. Then, in May of 1855, Edward repurchased the brick house. *The Hampshire and Franklin Express* congratulated him on returning "The Old Homestead" to the family.

The Homestead itself appears much the same as it did when Emily Dickinson lived here. However, when Dickinson was alive, the Homestead encompassed 14 acres and a barn. Emily Dickinson spent most of her life in this house; she was born here and she died here. In her conservatory, which attached to the southeast corner of the house, Dickinson grew many of the flowers that appear in poems such as "Distrustful of the gentian." The house itself provided fodder for poetry, which Dickinson transformed into such lines as "Eden is that old-fashioned House/We dwell in every day."

The Dickinson Homestead is owned by Amherst College. From early May through October, tours are available Wednesday through Saturday afternoons for $3.00 per person. From November until December 15, and during March and April, tours are conducted only on Wednesdays and Saturdays, and the Homestead is closed from December 15 until March 1. For an appointment to visit, call the Dickinson House at (413) 542-8161.

Allison Gosney
©'89

EMILY DICKINSON'S BEDROOM

Upstairs on the southwest corner of the Dickinson Homestead is Emily Dickinson's bedroom, the room in which she spent much of her time and wrote most of her poems. It was in this room, in a dresser drawer, that Lavinia Dickinson discovered many of the 1,775 poems her sister had written, some of which were sewn into small packets or "fascicles."

The central object of attention in the bedroom is, of course, the writing table. This was not Emily Dickinson's writing table, although we know she used one very similar to it. This table belonged to Susan Gilbert Dickinson, and stood in her bedroom at the Evergreens, which can be seen from the west windows. The bedroom's four windows, two facing Main Street and two facing west, played an important part in Dickinson's poems and letters. In fact, her written descriptions of the views out her windows, such as her poem, "By my window I have for scenery," helped to establish the location of her bedroom.

Beneath one of these windows is a basket with a curved handle. This basket is a Dickinson family piece, and this one or one like it was used by Emily Dickinson. It was her habit to bake gingerbread and other sweets, fill the basket with them, then, having brought the basket to her bedroom window, lower it down to the neighbor children below.

The small sleigh bed was donated by Mrs. Mason W. Tyler of Wellesley. Martha Dickinson Bianchi, Emily Dickinson's niece, gave the bed to the Tylers when she sold the Homestead. At that time she told them that the bed had belonged to Emily Dickinson. The child's chair and the cradle (in the hallway) were almost certainly items Dickinson used.

Other objects that were used by Emily Dickinson are the dress, the hat box, and the table clock. The white cotton dress is the property of the Amherst Historical Society, which was founded by Mabel Loomis Todd. Dickinson probably wore it in the last decade of her life. The hat box belonged to Dickinson's mother. Emily Dickinson may have used it when she travelled. The oval, mahogany Seth Thomas clock is said to have belonged to Dickinson. Tours of the bedroom are included in the tour of the Dickinson Homestead (see page 13).

MAP OF AMHERST

MASSACHUSETTS

LEGEND

1 - College Hall
2 - Dickinson Homestead
3 - Mount Holyoke
4 - First Church
5 - The Evergreens
6 - Helen Hunt Jackson House
7 - West Cemetery
8 - The Jones Library
9 - Site of Amherst Academy
10 - Frost Library
11 - Train Station
12 - Site of former North Pleasant St. Home

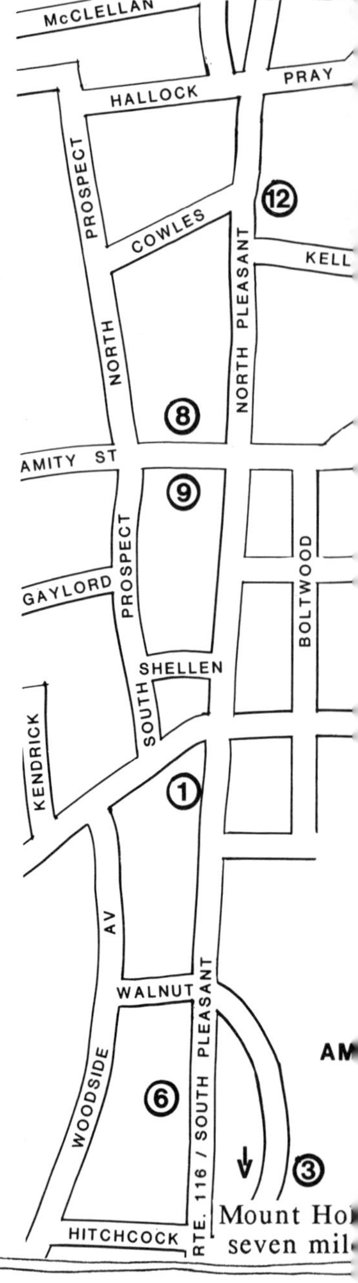

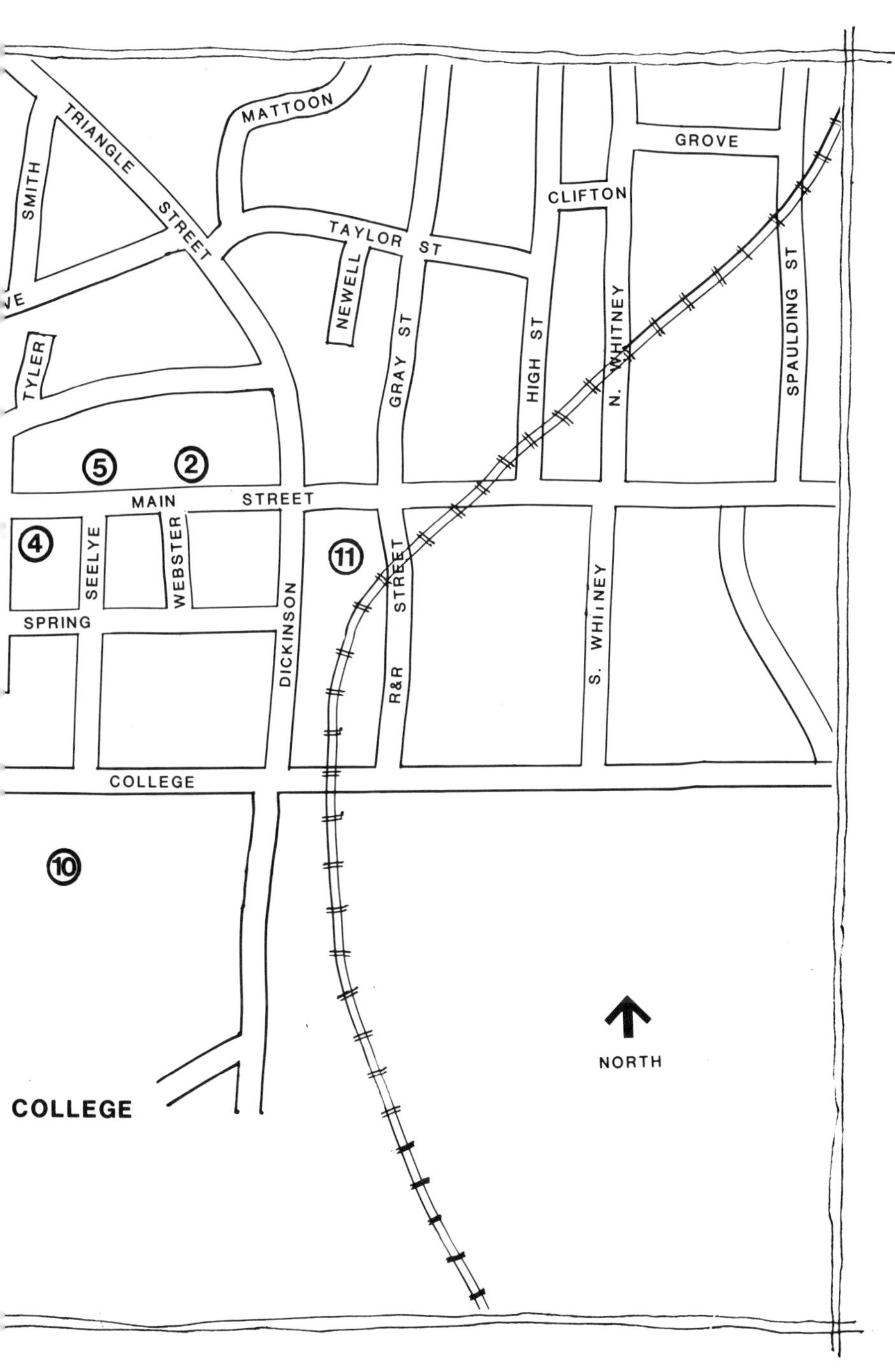
MATTOON
TRIANGLE
STREET
SMITH
GROVE
CLIFTON
TAYLOR ST
NEWELL
GRAY ST
HIGH ST
N. WHITNEY
SPAULDING ST
TYLER
5
2
MAIN
STREET
4
SEELYE
WEBSTER
11
R&R STREET
S. WHITNEY
SPRING
DICKINSON
COLLEGE
10
NORTH
COLLEGE

ALLISON GOSNEY
©'89

MOUNT HOLYOKE COLLEGE

About seven miles south of Amherst, in the town of South Hadley, lies Mount Holyoke College. Mount Holyoke was chartered in 1836 by Mary Lyon, as Mount Holyoke Female Seminary. Mary Lyon had been educated and taught school at various institutions, including Amherst Academy. With the help of early influences such as Edward Hitchcock and Joseph Emerson, Lyon started an institution to provide an education for women equal to that available to men.

Emily Dickinson first attended Mount Holyoke in the fall of 1847 (see Introduction page 6). She was pleased to pass the difficult entrance examination, (which many failed), and be admitted to the middle class. As one of the 235 women at the seminary, she attended classes, slept, dined, and exercised in the one building that served all the school's needs. That building burned to the ground in 1896, destroying all of the seminary except the library, which was housed in a separate building. In 1897 the school rebuilt its facilities, this time with several buildings, including Mary Lyon Hall, pictured opposite, which stands on the site of the original building where Emily Dickinson studied. The one photograph we have of her is a daguerreotype taken at Mount Holyoke in late 1847 or early 1848, probably at the "daguerrian's office" which had opened in December across the road from the seminary.

Dickinson attended the seminary for a total of ten months, or two terms. During that time she pursued a rigorous course of study which included chemistry, physiology, algebra, astronomy and rhetoric; she sang in one of the seminary choirs; and she enjoyed the surrounding landscape: the familiar views of Mount Holyoke and Mount Tom, the Connecticut River, a stream that ran through the grounds, and wildflowers growing in nearby meadows. Throughout the religious revival the school experienced in the 1840's and 50's, Dickinson never converted. Mount Holyoke has survived to become a distinguished center of women's secular education. Its library collects much Dickinson material, and scholars interested in the school's early history may want to consult the library archives. Tours and maps are available from the Admissions Office on Route 116 in South Hadley. Call (413) 538-2000 for more information.

ALLISON GOSNEY
©'89

THE EVERGREENS

The Evergreens, an Italian villa style house, is located at 214 Main Street, just west of the Dickinson Homestead. Edward Dickinson built it for his son Austin, and Austin's new bride, Susan Gilbert, hoping they would stay in Amherst. Austin and Susan were married July 1, 1856, in Geneva, New York. From then on, the Evergreens became the social center of Amherst. Susan was socially ambitious; at least once in 1857, she and Austin entertained Ralph Waldo Emerson.

Visits were frequent between the Evergreens and the Dickinson Homestead. At first Susan and Emily were close friends. They had attended Amherst Academy together, and during their friendship Emily shared over two hundred poems with Susan. Emily appreciated Susan's criticism--she wrote, "Your praise is good--because I *know* it *knows*"--but apparently only sought it in her early years. The last poem we know Emily showed Sue was, "Safe in Their Alabaster Chambers," of which there are two versions, one written in 1859 and one in 1861. The friendship between the two women cooled as Sue's interest was taken up by social activities and her own children. Further estrangement occurred during Austin's affair with Mabel Loomis Todd, which began in 1882 and lasted until his death in August 1895. During this time Austin visited Emily and Lavinia frequently, sometimes several times a day. Lavinia (and perhaps Emily) served as a kind of go-between for the pair. The book, *Austin and Mabel in Amherst*, details the affair.

When Emily Dickinson died, Susan Dickinson wrote the obituary which appeared in the *Springfield Republican* on May 18, 1886, painting what is now a familiar picture of Dickinson: ". . .The facts of her seclusion and her intellectual brilliancy were familiar Amherst traditions." Lavinia took Emily's poems to Susan, hoping she would help to publish them; however, Susan did nothing. Lavinia then turned to the only other suitable editor in Amherst--Mabel Loomis Todd--and the feud between the houses that began with Austin and Mabel's affair continued over Emily's poetry.

ALLISON GOSNEY
© '89

FIRST CHURCH

What the Dickinsons knew as First Church, the First Congregational Church of Amherst, now stands at 165 Main Street. Austin Dickinson presided over the construction and landscaping of this stone church in 1867-68. It was a big event in Amherst. The land had been purchased from the Montagues, distant cousins of the Dickinsons', and the site was almost directly across the street from the Evergreens and the Dickinson Homestead.

As a child, Emily Dickinson attended First Church with her family. At that time the congregation met in the building now known as College Hall (see page 11).

The construction of a new, permanent stone structure was not only an important event to the town; it was an important event to the Dickinson family. Edward Dickinson delivered the dedicatory address of the new church on September 23, 1868. Emily Dickinson's mother, Emily Norcross Dickinson, underwent conversion and joined the church in 1831. Her husband, Edward, joined the same day as their future daughter-in-law, Susan Gilbert: August 11, 1850. Emily's sister, Lavinia, also joined during the revival of 1850.

Of all her family, Emily alone resisted conversion. We know that she stopped going to church sometime in her late twenties, so she did not attend the new stone church. One of her most famous poems, "Some Keep the Sabbath Going to Church," eloquently presents her views on the subject. The proximity of the new church to her home, however, meant that she could hardly miss noticing it, and each of Dickinson's biographers repeat the story that one evening at the end of its construction, Emily went out with Austin to the edge of their property, to catch a glimpse of the new church.

In 1889 Austin Dickinson gave a speech during First Church's 150th anniversary celebration. Only three years after Emily Dickinson's death, Austin commented on the status of women in Amherst: "they have appeared above the surface in our last generation, and become a power."

First Church is open to the public every day from about 9 a.m. until about 5 p.m. Sunday services are held at 10 a.m. and visitors are welcome. First Church celebrated its 250th anniversary in 1989. Call (413) 253-3456 for more information.

ALLISON GOSNEY
© '89

HELEN HUNT JACKSON HOUSE

The Helen Hunt Jackson House is located at 249 South Pleasant Street across from the Amherst College campus. Jackson was born here in 1830, the same year as Emily Dickinson. The two attended school together in 1837, in a building which is still standing at 227 South Pleasant Street. When Jackson moved away, she and Dickinson lost touch until they were reunited in the early 1870's by a mutual friend, Thomas Wentworth Higginson. From then on the friendship proved strong. Jackson was one of the few people Dickinson shared poems with; she was, Cynthia Griffin Wolff writes, perhaps "her best reader."

By the 1870's Jackson was one of the country's leading women writers. Praised in print by Ralph Waldo Emerson, her poems and stories had appeared in journals such as the *Atlantic Monthly.* She was the only literary contemporary of Dickinson's to recognize her genius. In 1876 she wrote to Dickinson: "You are a great poet--and it is wrong to the day you live in, that you will not sing aloud. When you are what men call dead, you will be sorry you were so stingy."

Jackson's generosity extended beyond her letters--she repeatedly tried to get Dickinson's poems into print. In 1878 she succeeded, and Dickinson's "Success Is Counted Sweetest," was published anonymously in an anthology called *A Masque of Poets* by Roberts Brothers in Boston. Jackson then wrote her two most important works, *A Century of Dishonor* (1881), detailing the government's abuse of American Indians, and *Ramona* (1884), a best selling novel which dramatized the Indians' mistreatment. Both works had a serious impact on the country and brought about reforms. *Ramona* went through more than 300 editions in English, and is still in print today.

One year after its publication, Helen Hunt Jackson died. Shortly before her death, she had asked to be Emily Dickinson's literary executor, still intent on publishing her poems. Stricken by the loss, Dickinson wrote three poems in memory of Jackson, which she sent in letters to Thomas Wentworth Higginson: "Not Knowing When the Dawn Will Come," "Of Glory Not a Beam Is Left," and "The Immortality She Gave." Purchased by Amherst College in 1921, the Helen Hunt Jackson House is now a private residence, marked by a plaque.

ALLISON GOSHEY
©'89

WEST CEMETERY

West Cemetery is located off of Triangle Street in Amherst. The cemetery is surrounded by downtown buildings now, but in Emily Dickinson's time only a long meadow divided it from the Dickinson Homestead. The cemetery contains the graves of Edward and Emily Norcross Dickinson, Emily's parents; Lavinia Dickinson, Emily's sister; and Emily Dickinson herself.

Emily Dickinson died on Saturday, May 15, 1886. She was buried on Wednesday, May 19, 1886. She was laid out in her customary white dress, in a simple white casket adorned by violets and pine boughs. She was 55.

By sitting at deathbed "watches" and nursing ill friends and family, Dickinson had been in close contact with death for years. Many of her most famous poems, such as "Because I could not stop for death," address death.

Emily Dickinson's pallbearers were the six men who worked on her father's grounds: Thomas Kelley, Dennis Scannell, Stephen Sullivan, Patrick Ward, Daniel Moynihan, and Dennis Cashman. They carried her out the back door of the Homestead, through the field to the cemetery. Thomas Wentworth Higginson was at the funeral; he read from an Emily Bronte's poem. The pastor of the Congregational Church read from Scriptures.

Emily Dickinson was buried next to her mother and father. The Dickinson graves are centrally placed in the cemetery, inside a wrought iron fence, beneath a cedar tree.

Emily Dickinson died from complications of Bright's disease, a kidney ailment. She lapsed into a coma on May 13, 1886, and never regained consciousness. The last piece of her writing we have is a letter from her to her favorite cousins, Frances and Louise Norcross, in Cambridge. It says simply,

Little Cousins,
Called back.
Emily.

The gravestone on Dickinson's grave is not the original one; lost or damaged, no one knows for sure what happened to it. The stones adorning the Dickinson plot were placed there by Emily's niece, Martha Dickinson Bianchi. It was she who chose the two words of that last letter as Emily Dickinson's epitaph.

ALLISON GOSNEY
© '89

THE JONES LIBRARY

The Jones Library, located at 43 Amity Street in downtown Amherst, was dedicated in 1928. A stone building with gambrel roof and gables, it contains nearly 100,000 volumes. The Jones Library is the library for the town of Amherst, free and open to the public. It is also an invaluable resource for anyone interested in Emily Dickinson.

The library's extensive Emily Dickinson Collection is housed in the Emily Dickinson Room. The interesting collection is well presented and serves the needs of the serious researcher as well as the general public. Nearly 7,000 items relating to Emily Dickinson's life and poetry reside there. The items range from a bonnet and some buttons Emily Dickinson wore to the typewriter Mabel Loomis Todd used to edit the first edition of Emily Dickinson's poetry. There are original manuscript materials and letters, first editions and later printings of Emily Dickinson's poems. The collection also includes secondary research materials. Several display cases exhibit Dickinson memorabilia, including a model of Emily Dickinson's bedroom.

The Special Collections Department boasts an outstanding collection of material on Amherst's history, including 50,000 photographs, maps, town records, early newspapers, and works by Amherst authors, such as Emily Dickinson's friend Helen Hunt Jackson. Daniel Lombardo is the Curator of Special Collections. He himself has published an account of Amherst history in *Tales of Amherst: A Look Back*. Visitors may want to explore the library's collection of materials relating to another great American poet, Robert Frost, in the Robert Frost Room.

The Jones Library Special Collections is open Monday through Friday from 9 a.m. until 5 p.m., and on Tuesdays until 9 p.m. Saturdays Special Collections opens from 10 a.m. until 5 p.m. Visitors are welcome, but those interested in conducting research in Special Collections are encouraged to make an appointment with the Curator. A few items are available for sale, including a poster and postcards of Emily Dickinson. The telephone number is (413) 256-4090.

ALLISON GOSNEY
©'89

THE FROST LIBRARY

The Robert Frost Library is a modern brick building centrally located on the campus of Amherst College. It was dedicated in 1963 as a memorial to the late poet, an Amherst resident and Amherst College professor. President John F. Kennedy spoke at the building's dedication. The Frost Library serves as the main library for Amherst College and contains over 600,000 volumes.

One of the country's most extensive collections of Dickinson material is housed here. Holdings range from all published material about Emily Dickinson, such as poems, letters, biographies, and critical studies, to original manuscripts, artifacts such as maps, photographs, paintings and drawings, and other memorabilia. As many members of the Dickinson family were involved in the early history of Amherst College, the Frost Library provides an excellent resource for research and reading about all of the Dickinsons. Here one can trace the editing and eventual publication of all of Emily Dickinson's poems, from the efforts of Susan Gilbert Dickinson and Mabel Loomis Todd, through their children, Martha Dickinson Bianchi and Millicent Todd Bingham, to the definitive edition of *The Complete Poems* compiled by Thomas H. Johnson in 1955.

The Archives and Special Collections of the library are located downstairs from the main floor. Here the college preserves original, handwritten copies of Dickinson's poems, the original letters Dickinson wrote to family and friends, and first editions of the poems. The only photograph of Dickinson--the daguerreotype taken while she was at Mount Holyoke--is preserved here.

Special Collections welcomes the public to view their two glass cases exhibiting material about Dickinson and Frost, and to browse through their extensive collection of Dickinson books, which are stored in locked cases but available upon request. A few items, such as cards and a copy of the daguerreotype, are for sale. For the purpose of preservation, however, access to manuscript materials is severely limited. Special Collections is open Monday through Friday from 8:30 a.m. until 4:30 p.m. For more information contact the library at (413) 542-2212.

BIBLIOGRAPHY

Many books and articles have been written about Emily Dickinson. The following list includes those which make extensive reference to her life in Amherst.

Bianchi, Martha Dickinson. *Emily Dickinson Face to Face.* Boston: Houghton Mifflin Co., 1932.

_____. *The Life and Letters of Emily Dickinson.* Boston: Houghton Mifflin Co., 1924.

Bingham, Millicent Todd. *Ancestors' Brocades: The Literary Debut of Emily Dickinson.* New York: Harper and Brothers, 1945.

_____. *Emily Dickinson's Home: Letters of Edward Dickinson and his Family.* New York: Harper and Brothers, 1955.

Franklin, R. W., ed. *The Master Letters of Emily Dickinson.* Amherst, Mass.: Amherst College Press, 1986.

_____. *The Manuscript Books of Emily Dickinson.* Cambridge, Mass.: Harvard University Press, 1981.

Johnson, Thomas H. *The Complete Poems of Emily Dickinson.* Boston: Little Brown and Co., 1960.

_____. *Emily Dickinson: Selected Letters.* Cambridge, Mass.: Harvard University Press, 1971.

Lombardo, Daniel. *Tales of Amherst.* Amherst, Mass.: The Jones Library, Inc., 1986.

Longsworth, Polly. *Austin and Mabel.* New York: Holt Rinehart Winston, 1984.

Sewall, Richard. *The Life of Emily Dickinson.* New York: Farrar, Straus, Giroux, 1980.

Wolff, Cynthia Griffin. *Emily Dickinson.* New York: Addison-Wesley Publishing Co., 1988.